300 Sermon Outlines from the New Testament

300
SERMON OUTLINES
from the
NEW TESTAMENT

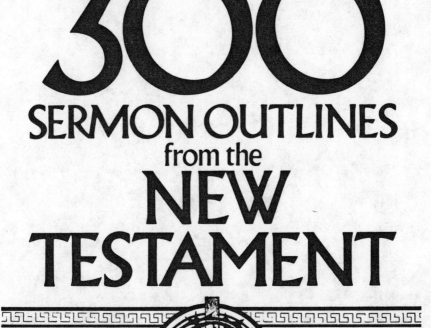

William H. Smitty

BROADMAN PRESS
Nashville, Tennessee

4222-46
ISBN: 0-8054-2246-3

Dewey Decimal Classification: 225
Subject heading: BIBLE. N.T.—SERMONS
Library of Congress Catalog Card Number: 8186666
Printed in the United States of America

Preface

300 Sermon Outlines from the New Testament has been put together as a sequel to my book, *300 Sermon Outlines from the Old Testament*.

It is presented with the prayer that it will be beneficial to those seeking Bible-centered material for sermons and spiritual talks. I trust that these outlines will become a helpful basis for deeper investigation and proclamation of God's Word. If these outlines direct hearts and minds better to prepare for the sacred time spent behind the pulpit, they will have served their purpose. They are sent forth with the hope that they will cultivate just such a mood.

WILLIAM H. SMITTY

Contents

300 Sermon Outlines from the New Testament

MATTHEW

The Other Side of Christmas *(Matt. 2:16-18)*
   I. There are those who are at work to destroy the
       truth revealed by the event.
  II. There are facts revealed by the event which, unless
      acknowledged, will harden the heart to truth.
 III. The event is not always a time of glimmer and joy;
      it can also be a time of suffering for many.
     A. The needy
     B. The afflicted, etc.

A Divine Invitation to Service *(Matt. 4:19)*
   I. Invitation of a Divine Person
     ("And *he* saith unto them.")
  II. Invitation to a challenging prospect
     ("*Follow* me.")
 III. Invitation to a rewarding purpose
     ("I will make you *fishers of men*.")

Blessings of the Beatitudes *(Matt. 5:1-12)*
   I. The Blessings of Humility
     A. Spiritual vision (v. 3)
     B. Divine comfort (v. 4)
     C. Promised inheritance (v. 5)
  II. The Blessings of Holiness
     A. Spiritual sustenance (v. 6)
     B. Divine mercy (v. 7)
     C. Personal encounter with God (v. 8)
 III. The Blessings of Happiness
     A. Spiritual sonship (v. 9)

B. Divine reward (v. 10)

C. Permanent provision (vv. 11-12)

The Christian's Prayer Life *(Matt. 6:6)*

I. It is assumed that prayer will be a natural part of the Christian experience.

("When thou prayest")

II. It is assumed that the Christian will have a place of prayer.

("Enter into thy closet.")

III. It is assumed that the Christian will be very personal in his praying.

("Shut thy door.")

IV. It is assumed that the Christian will desire the fellowship of prayer.

("Pray to thy Father.")

V. It is a promise from God that he will reward such praying.

("Father will reward thee")

The Savior's Plea for Loyalty *(Matt. 6:24-33)*

I. The plea should be honored when considering the speaker.

A. As Lord he has the right to expect loyalty.

B. As Savior he set the perfect example in his loyalty to God's will.

C. As God in flesh he could speak from experience, having been tempted to serve mammon and overcome.

II. The plea should be honored when considering the two choices (v. 24).

A. God always gives us a choice.

B. Divided loyalties always result in unfaithful-
ness.
C. Loyalty to Christ calls for nothing less than
total servitude.
III. The plea should be honored when considering the
results.
A. It is a mistake to put necessities of life ahead of
loyalty to Christ.
B. Loyalty abolishes overanxiousness about life's
needs.
C. Loyalty guarantees assurance of God's provision
in life's needs.

Successful Praying *(Matt. 7:7-8)*
I. Prayer is the blessed privilege of the saints.
A. We have but to ask and receive.
B. We have but to seek and find.
C. We have but to knock and to have the door of
God's heart opened unto us.
II. Answered prayer is the promised reward.
A. The promise assumes a genuine relationship
with God.
B. The promise assumes a proper fellowship with
God.
C. The promise assumes proper wisdom in pray-
ing.
III. Persistence is the key to successful praying.
("Ask," "Seek," "Knock.")

Christ, the Gate to Life *(Matt. 7:13-14)*
I. The wide gate to destruction has always been to
man's disadvantage.

II. Christ, the gate to life, was sent to give man a choice.

III. Christ, the gate to life, was sent to give man the advantage.

Builders *(Matt. 7:21-29)*

I. Jesus Describes a Wise Builder (vv. 24-25).
  A. One who follows instructions
  B. One who chooses a proper foundation
  C. One who is not foolish enough to ignore the importance of the above
II. Jesus Describes a Foolish Builder (vv. 26-27).
  A. One who ignores instructions
  B. One who builds on a weak foundation
  C. One who suffers loss for trusting in a plan of his own devising

A Simple Invitation to Salvation *(Matt. 11:28)*

I. Notice the simplicity of Christ's invitation.
  ("Come unto me")
II. Notice the general character of those included in Christ's simple invitation.
  ("All ye that labour and are heavy laden")
III. Notice the great truth revealed in Christ's simple invitation.
  ("I will give you rest")

Sign Seekers *(Matt. 12:38-42)*

I. Sign seekers are truth rejecters.
  A. "Adulterous generation" (v. 39)
  B. Refers to religious apostasy

14

II. Sign seekers are easily deceived.
  A. "Evil . . . generation" (v. 39)
  B. Refers to following teachings based upon man's interpretation of truth
III. Sign seekers are faithless people.
  A. Contrasted to faith of "men of Nineveh" (v. 41) and of "queen of [Sheba]" (v. 42)
  B. Faith goes beyond signs and seeks Jesus (vv. 39*b* -40). (Note reference to light from God's Word pinpointing truth revealed in Jesus, v. 40.)

Reformation Without Salvation *(Matt. 12:43-45)*
  I. Here is an unsaved man who attempted to reform.
    A. The unclean spirit was not cast out but left of himself.
    B. The unclean spirit returned at will.
  II. Here is a reformed man who was helpless against the power of sin.
    A. He left the house empty after the unclean spirit had gone out of him (that is, he did not put Christ in the empty house).
    B. The house still belonged to the unclean spirit. ("I will return into my house.")
  III. Here is a religious man who is the worse off for it.
    A. "Swept, and garnished" by false righteousness
    B. Possessed by greater wickedness in the end

Christian Fellowship *(Matt. 18:19-20)*
Introduction
The gathering of God's people for fellowship and worship is taught and assumed in the Scriptures. Three things

15

stand out, therefore, when we think of Christian fellowship.

I. Togetherness
   A. Togetherness implies more in the Scriptures than merely coming together in an assembly.
      1. Implies oneness (in one accord)
      2. Implies harmony (no contention)
   B. Without togetherness any joint effort in the church is impossible.

II. Love
   A. It is love which creates a desire for fellowship.
      1. Love for God
      2. Love of Christ within us
      3. Love for one another
   B. It is love which preserves the unity of fellowship (1 Cor. 13:4-7).

III. Growth
   A. Division is a sign of immature Christianity (1 Cor. 3:1-3).
   B. Unity is a sign of spiritual maturity (Col. 3:8-10).

"What Lack I Yet?" *(Matt. 19:16-22).*

I. This was the cry of a rich man (v. 22). ("For he had great possessions.")
II. This was the cry of a religious man (v. 20). ("All these have I kept from my youth up.")
III. This was the cry of a reformed man (v. 16). ("What good thing shall I do?")
IV. This was the cry of a rebellious man (v. 22). ("He went away sorrowful.")

An Example of Unstable Hearts *(Matt. 21:4-11; 27:20-26)*
  I. The Unstable Condition of the Crowd
    A. The two cries
      1. "Hosanna" (21:9)
      2. "Crucify" (27:22-23)
    B. The two choices
      1. Christ
      2. Barabbas
    C. The two changing factors
      1. False teachers (27:20)
      2. Mob violence (27:23)
  II. The Unstable Faith of the Crowd
    A. Had faith in Christ when they thought that he would immediately rule as the king over Israel
    B. When the chips were down for Jesus their faith proved untrue
  III. The Unstable Enthusiasm of the Crowd
    A. Was based upon hope of personal gain
    B. Was based upon misinformation (Disregarded scriptural truth altogether)
    C. Was based upon emotionalism without spiritual foundation
Conclusion (See Jer. 17:9.)

The Word Supreme *(Matt. 24:35)*
  I. Here Christ proclaims the supernaturalness of the Word.
  II. Here Christ proclaims the eminence of the Word.
  III. Here Christ proclaims the immutability of the Word.

IV. Here Christ proclaims the indestructibility of the
    Word.

The Contents of the Cup *(Matt. 26:26-29)*
Introduction
Inside the communion cup are represented these four
things
    I. The atonement provided by Christ (v. 28)
      ("This is my blood . . . which is shed . . . for the
      remission of sins.")
    II. Those for whom Christ died (v. 28)
      ("For many")
    III. The New Covenant (v. 28)
      ("This is my blood of the new testament")
    IV. The assurance of our security in Christ (v. 29)
      ("Until that day when I drink it new with you in my
      Father's kingdom")

Backseat Religion *(Matt. 26:31-35,56-58,69-75)*
Introduction
In these Scriptures we see Peter, the avowed follower of
Christ, becoming a weak man who follows "afar off."
    I. This truth demonstrates the danger of allowing a
       distance to develop in our fellowship with
       Christ.
    II. This truth demonstrates the danger of an overconfi-
       dence in our ability alone to overcome the
       world.
    III. This truth demonstrates the danger of sitting down
       with the enemies of Christ.
    IV. This truth demonstrates that backseat religion is a
       very dangerous place for the child of God to be.

The Big, Big Question *(Matt. 27:22)*
("What shall I do then with Jesus who is called Christ?")
    I. The Personal Decision
    II. The Person of Debate
    III. The Problem Declared
    IV. The Principle Deduced

The Tragic Answer to a Great Question *(Matt. 27:22)*
("They all say unto him, Let him be crucified.")
    I. Consider the person identified by the question.
    II. Consider the personal confrontation presented by the question.
    III. Consider the peril resulting from the answer given to the question.
    IV. Consider the privilege made possible by responding wisely to the question.

The World's Most Notable Event *(Matt. 28:1-10)*
    I. The Notable Earthquake (vv. 2-4)
        A. A supernatural event
        B. A supernatural revelation
           (That Christ was not there)
    II. The Notable Message (vv. 5-7)
        A. Delivered by an angel
        B. To be propagated by man
    III. The Notable Appearance (v. 9)
        A. The resurrected Lord
        B. The revelation calls for devotion

How to Become Better Stewards of the Gospel *(Matt. 28:19-20)*
  I. Know the Gospel (2 Tim. 2:15).
 II. Live the Gospel (Matt. 5:6).
III. Love the Gospel (Ps. 119:34).
IV. Give the Gospel (Ps. 107:2).

MARK

"Follow Me" *(Mark 1:16-20)*
   I. Christ can conform natural skills for use in his service.
   II. Serving Christ often calls for the forsaking of one profession to enter another.
   III. Serving Christ often calls for the forsaking of former relationships in order to follow him.

Tormented Sinners *(Mark 5:1-8)*
   I. The sinner is tormented because of the insanity of sin.
   II. The sinner is tormented because of the fetters of sin.
   III. The sinner is tormented because of the unhappiness of sin.
   IV. Christ allows the torment to deliver the sinner from the power of sin.

Saved and Secure *(Mark 5:22-34)*
   I. The Lingering Disease
      (Compare to sin.)
   II. The Sensitive Savior
      (Consider Christ's reaction to the sinner's touch of faith.)
   III. The Permanent Results
      (Conclude with the believing sinner's security in Christ.)

Christ the Restorer *(Mark 8:22-26)*
  I. For needy men to receive the touch of Christ, they must be brought to him.
  II. Jesus will lead those who are willing to be led.
  III. Jesus never leaves those seeking him to become victims of half-way measures.
  IV. Jesus never deals with one's life without giving clear instructions for the future (v. 26).

Christ's Great Paradox *(Mark 8:34-36)*
  I. To Deny Is to Affirm (v. 34).
  II. To Lose Is to Save (v. 35).
  III. To Profit Is to Forfeit (v. 36).

The Soul Gambler *(Mark 8:36-37)*
  I. The soul is man's most valuable asset.
  II. To gamble the soul on the stock market of worldliness is very foolish, for there is nothing to gain in light of eternity.
  III. In soul gambling there is really no contest, for Satan has the deck stacked in his favor.

How Children Come to Jesus *(Mark 10:13-16)*
  I. With simple faith
  II. With less appetite for sin
  III. With a pure heart of love
  IV. Without a hindering pride
  V. Without the preconceived notions that often hinder adults
  VI. With a whole life to give to him

Four Decisions As Revealed at the Triumphal Entry of Christ *(Mark 11:1-11,* compare following chapters*)*
- I. The decision gladly to receive him
- II. The decision to be skeptical of him
- III. The decision to hate and reject him
- IV. The decision to scorn him

Three Halfheartedness Danger Zones *(Mark 12:30)*
- I. In Our Worship (Ex. 8:25)
- II. In Our Service (Ex. 10:11)
- III. In Our Compromising (Ex. 10:24)

LUKE

Appraisal of a Great Man *(Luke 1:1-15)*
   I. God's Appraisal (Mal. 3:1)
     ("My messenger")
  II. Christ's Appraisal (Matt. 11:11)
     ("There hath not risen a greater than John the Baptist")
 III. Herod's Appraisal (Mark 6:11)
     ("A just man and an holy")
 IV. The Angel's Appraisal (Luke 1:15)
     ("He shall be great in the sight of the Lord")

Mary, Example of Christian Womanhood *(Luke 1:26-38)*
   I. Mary demonstrates the maternal nature of Christian womanhood.
     A. Called to receive a son as a charge from God
     B. Called to give a son as a service to mankind
  II. Mary demonstrates the spiritual nature of Christian womanhood.
     A. Her love bond with God
       ("Handmaid," v. 38*a*)
     B. Her quiet inner praise of God
       ("My soul doth magnify the Lord" (v. 46)
 III. Mary demonstrated the submissive nature of Christian womanhood.
     A. As in her beginning (Eve), so ought woman to rediscover the call to obedience.
     B. As Mary submitted to God's will in this matter, so ought Christian women to say, "Be it unto me according to thy word" (v. 38*b*).

An Outstanding Witness for Christ *(Luke 2:25-32)*
I. A man who found Christ according to the Scriptures.
II. A man who proclaimed Christ as the Savior of the Scriptures.
III. A Man Who Glorified Christ As the Fulfillment of the Scriptures

A Sinner's Approach to Jesus *(Luke 5:12)*
I. With Spiritual Vision
("Who seeing Jesus")
II. With Humble Repentance
("Fell on his face")
III. With Desire for Divine Help
("Besought him")
IV. With Faith
("Thou canst")

Prevailing Principles of Divine Deliverance *(Luke 5:31-32)*
I. The principle of demand and supply
II. The principle of personal awareness of human inability
III. The principle of submission to the healing process

Four Notable Men *(Luke 10:30-35)*
I. The Hurting, Helpless Man
II. The Unconcerned, Priestly Man
III. The Curious, Religious Man
IV. The Despised, Benevolent Man

Seeds of a Foolish Farmer *(Luke 12:16-20)*
  I. The seeds he sowed pertained to material life only.
  II. The seeds he sowed obscured his vision of impending death.
  III. The seeds he sowed destroyed his hope of eternal life.

The Prepared, Unprepared Man *(Luke 12:16-20)*
  I. He was prepared to live physically, but unprepared to live spiritually.
  II. He was prepared to die financially, but unprepared for death spiritually.
  III. He was prepared to reap an earthly harvest, but unprepared to share heaven's riches.

The Proper Christian Outlook *(Luke 12:23,28)*
  I. Our hope is based upon eternal values.
     ("Life is more than meat," v. 23*a*.)
  II. Our chief investment is in Christian service.
      ("The body is more than raiment," v. 23*b*.)
  III. Our faith is grounded upon God's promise of provision.
       ("How much more will he clothe you?" v. 28.)

Willing Discipleship *(Luke 14:25-30)*
  I. Nothing must come before him, not even family (v. 26).
  II. Nothing must become too great to bear for him (v. 27).
  III. Nothing must be done halfheartedly in service to him (vv. 28-30).

Three Parables, Three Lessons *(Luke 15:1-32)*

    I. In the first parable we should become those who rejoice when the lost are saved (v. 6).

    II. In the second parable we should become the lighted candle (v. 8).

    ("Ye are the light of the world")

    III. In the third parable we can take one of two positions:

        A. The position of servitude (vv. 22-23).

        B. The position of the jealous brother (vv. 28-30).

A Prodigal's Predicament *(Luke 15:11-16)*

    I. Humanistic Rationality

    II. Hasty Rebellion

    III. Harmful Riotousness

    IV. Heathenish Ruin

Finding God *(Luke 15:17-24)*

    I. Spiritual Reasoning

    II. Speedy Return

    III. Sorrowful Repentance

    IV. Saving Reunion

    V. Sanctioned Rejoicing

A Backslider's Steps to Ruin *(Luke 15:11-16)*

    I. Blundering Decision (v. 12)

    II. Bold Departure (v. 13*a*)

    III. Bad Company (v. 13*b*)

    IV. Baffling Circumstances (v. 14)

    V. Besetting Outcome (vv. 15-16)

When Faithfulness Is Wrong *(Luke 15:25-30)*
The elder brother proved his attitude about faithfulness
to be wrong in at least three ways (v. 29):
    I. He felt that it should excuse a spirit of haughtiness.
    II. He felt that it should excuse a spirit of hatefulness.
    III. He felt that it should excuse a spirit of heartless-
        ness.

The Bad, Good Guy *(Luke 15:25-30)*
    I. Bad because of an overestimation of his goodness
    II. Bad because of an unforgiving attitude toward his
        brother's badness
    III. Bad because of an unloving spirit of condemnation
        toward the love of his father for the prodigal
        brother
    IV. Bad because he demanded grace on the basis of
        goodness while denying forgiveness for his
        brother on the basis of grace

The Revelation of Hell *(Luke 16:19-26)*
    I. The Reality of Hell.
    II. The Regrets of Hell.
    III. The Ravishes of Hell.
    IV. The Lack of Redemption for Those in Hell.

A Witness Beyond Death *(Luke 16:19-31)*
    I. The presence of Lazarus in Abraham's bosom be-
        came a witness against the self-seeking life of
        the rich man (v. 23).

II. The secure condition of Lazarus became a witness to the rich man of his own permanent state of hopelessness (v. 24).

III. The comfortable state of Lazarus became a witness to the rich man of the justice of God (v. 25).

IV. The righteous reward of Lazarus became a witness to the rich man of the validity of faith in the Scriptures (vv. 27-31).

The Most Foolish Prayer in the Bible *(Luke 16:27-31)*

I. It was the prayer of a man who had shunned the godly life and was now in hell as his just judgment.

(How foolish—he prayed too late.)

II. He prayed for God to make a special exception in regard to the need of his brothers to be saved.

(How foolish—God is no respecter of persons in regard to the way of salvation.)

III. He asked that his brothers be convinced of their need for God by a method which left out faith in the teachings of the Scriptures.

(How foolish—God's Word is always the basis of his dealings with mankind.)

Three Great Truths in a Well-Known Story *(Luke 18:10-14)*

I. The False Security of the Pharisee

II. The True Guilt of the Publican

III. The Great Justice of a Loving God

The Confession of a Sinner *(Luke 18:13-14)*

 I. His manner of approach to God was an Admission of guilt.

 ("Standing afar off.")

 II. His manner of approach to God was a demonstration of genuine humility.

 ("Would not so much as lift up his eyes unto heaven.")

 III. His manner of approach to God was an act of repentance.

 ("Smote upon his breast.")

 IV. His manner of approach to God constituted a prayer of faith which denied any personal merit.

 ("God be merciful to me a sinner.")

 V. His manner of approach to God resulted in his justification by God's grace.

 ("I tell you, this man went down to his house justified.")

Four Reasons for Observing the Lord's Supper *(Luke 22:17-20)*

 I. It is the means of declaring our faith in the victorious death of Christ.

 ("For even Christ our passover is sacrificed for us," 1 Cor. 5:17)

 II. It is the means of strengthening the bonds of Christian fellowship.

 ("Take this, and divide it among yourselves," Luke 22:17)

 III. It is the means of expressing obedience to Christ's command.

 ("This do in remembrance of me," Luke 22:19)

IV. It is a means by which Christians can examine themselves (1 Cor. 11:27-30).

The Day Christ Died *(Luke 23:18-48)*
I. A condemned criminal was set free (v. 25).
II. A seeking sinner was saved (vv. 42-43).
III. A convicted centurion believed (v. 47).
IV. A temperamental thief was lost (v. 39).
V. A calamitous crowd mourned (v. 48).

Three Lessons from an Enlightened, Rebellious Sinner *(Luke 23:33,39)*
I. To be near Christ is not salvation.
II. To want to be saved is not salvation.
III. To address Christ, even while dying, is not necessarily salvation.

The Bible's Most Profound Prayer *(Luke 23:34, Jesus prayed, "Father, forgive them")*
I. It was a prayer for his murderers.
II. It was a prayer for his mockers.
III. It was a prayer for his tempters.
IV. It was a prayer for his skeptics.
V. It was a prayer for his doubters.
VI. It was a prayer for his rejecters.
VII. It was, above all, a prayer of compassion.
   ("For they know not what they do")

How a Thief Came to Jesus *(Luke 23:39-42)*
I. He came with a clear recognition of personal guilt.
II. He came empty handed.
   A. He could offer no good works.
   B. He could offer no religiosity.

III. He came with a holy fear of God.

IV. He came in an attitude of repentance.

V. He came in total faith.

The Lamb Between Two Thieves *(Luke 23:39-43)*

   I. The Dead, Dying Thief (v. 39)

     A. Alive physically but dead spiritually

     B. Dying in the presence of the Lamb of God to face eternal retribution

  II. The Divine, Dying Son (v. 43)

     A. Divine, therefore Savior

     B. Dying physically that men might live spiritually

 III. The Discriminating, Dying Thief (vv. 40-42)

     A. Discriminating judgment of self brought spiritual life.

     B. Death, therefore, was a door to everlasting life for this thief who trusted in Christ.

JOHN

The Revelation of the Word *(John 1:1-3,14)*
I. In Glory
II. In Creation
III. In Flesh
IV. In Manifestation
V. In Grace and Truth

Seven-Point Description of Christ *(John 1:1-5,12,14)*
I. Christ the Alpha (vv. 1-2)
II. Christ the Incarnate Word (vv. 1,14)
III. Christ the Creator (v. 3)
IV. Christ the Means of Spiritual Life (v. 4a)
V. Christ the Light of Men (v. 4b)
VI. Christ the Destroyer of Sin (v. 5)
VII. Christ the Savior (v. 12)

Come Alive *(John 1:4-5)*
I. This is a Call to come out of spiritual darkness and death (v. 5).
II. This is a Call to come into new life in Christ (v. 4a).
III. This is a Call to come into the full illumination of God's light (v. 4b).

The Perfect Plan of Salvation *(John 1:12)*
I. The Way Made Possible
("As many as received him")
II. The Way Is Powerful
("To them gave he power")

III. The Way Is Positive
("To become the sons of God")
IV. The Way Is Prepared
("His name")

Salvation's Greatness *(John 1:29)*
I. The Great Need
("Sin of the world")
II. The Great Sacrifice
("Lamb of God")
III. The Great Results
("Taketh away the sin")

An Ancient Law Fulfilled *(John 1:29)*
I. The Need: A Sacrifice
("The sin of the world")
II. The Sacrifice Provided: Christ
("Behold the Lamb of God")
III. The Results: Salvation
("Taketh away the sin of the world")

John's Word Picture of Christ *(John 1:29-33)*
I. The Savior of the World (v. 29)
II. The Preeminent One (vv. 30,34)
III. The Messiah of Israel (v. 31)
IV. The Anointed One (v. 32)
V. The Bestower of the Holy Spirit (v. 33)

Birth in the Spirit *(John 3:5)*
I. Natural birth, though a great miracle, leaves us an
incomplete creation because of original sin.

II. Spiritual birth, though a great possibility, cannot penetrate an unwilling heart.

III. The kingdom of God, though a great attainment, cannot be gained without a second birth.

Saved or Condemned: A Choice *(John 3:18)*
   I. The Individualism Involved
      ("He that")
  II. The Faith Required
     ("Believeth on him")
 III. The Promise Stated
     ("Is not condemned")
 IV. The Warning Given
    ("He that believeth not is condemned already")
  V. The Reason Given
     ("Hath not believed")

Pardon or Perdition *(John 3:36)*
   I. This verse clearly states the position of the pardoned sinner.
     ("Hath everlasting life")
  II. This verse clearly states the position of the unpardoned sinner.
     ("Wrath of God abideth on him")
 III. This verse clearly states the perdition of the unpardoned sinner.
     ("Shall not see life")

Choosing Life or Death *(John 3:36)*
   I. The Prospect ("He that")
   The sinner

II. The Possibility ("Everlasting life" and "He that believeth")
Faith
III. The Petitioner ("The Son")
Christ
IV. The Privilege ("He that believeth on the Son" and "He that believeth not the Son")
Free choice

Soul-Searching Advice *(John 5:39)*

I. To know scriptural truth we must diligently search the Scriptures.
II. What we think personally about the Scriptures may not be a correct interpretation.
III. To falsely interpret the Scriptures can close the door to eternal life.

Christ, the Answer to Religious Confusion *(John 6:66-69)*

I. Two Great Questions
   A. The question Jesus asked (v. 67)
      ("Will ye also go away?")
   B. The question Peter asked (v. 68)
      ("Lord, to whom shall we go"—Who else holds the answer to truth?)
II. Two Great Answers
   A. Christ, the only person with the answer (v. 68*b*)
      ("Thou hast the words of eternal life")
   B. Faith, the substance of the answer (v. 69)
      ("And we believe and are sure that thou art the Christ, the Son of the living God")

Christ's Appraisal of the Scriptures *(John 7:38)*
   I. Christ authenticates the Scriptures.
   II. Christ acclaims himself as the Savior of the Scriptures.
   III. Christ announces the benefits of faith in the Scriptures.
   IV. Christ answered the skeptics of the Scriptures.

The Greatest Words Ever Spoken *(John 7:46)*
Introduction
(Consider the seven last words of Christ as uttered from the cross, "Never man spake like this man")
   I. Utterances of Suffering
      A. "I Thirst" (John 19:28).
      B. "My God, my God, why hast thou forsaken me?" (Matt. 27:46).
   II. Utterances of Compassion
      A. "Father, forgive them" (Luke 23:34).
      B. "To-day shalt thou be with me in paradise" (Luke 23:43).
      C. "Behold thy mother!" (John 19:27).
   III. Utterances of Victory
      A. "It is finished" (John 19:30).
      B. "Father, into thy hands I commend my spirit" (Luke 23:46).

Christ's Words *(John 8:51)*
   I. Christ's words are true words.
   II. Christ's words are the only source of hope for lost mankind.
   III. Christ's words ought to be kept.
   IV. Obedience to Christ's words is a life or death

decision which each individual alone can make.

Privileged Fellowship *(John 9:31)*
I. God withholds his fellowship from sinners.
II. God Bestows his fellowship upon the saved.
III. God expects those blessed with his fellowship to express their gratitude in his service.

The Door *(John 10:9)*
I. A door is for opening.
(Faith alone opens the door to salvation.)
II. A door is for closing.
(Faith gives assurance that the old, condemned life is left behind when one steps through the door to salvation.)
III. A door is for locking.
(Faith brings security to those who enter the door to salvation.)
IV. A door is for stability.
(Faith will establish those who step through the door to salvation in sound, biblical teaching.)

John's Four-Verse Gospel of Christ's Life *(John 10:14)*
I. John 10:10 (Born for a purpose)
("I am come that they might have life")
II. John 12:32 (Crucified for a purpose)
("Lifted up . . . will draw all men unto me")
III. John 14:2 (Ascended for a purpose)
("I go to prepare a place for you")
IV. John 14:3 (Returning for a purpose)

("I will come again, and receive you unto myself")

A Great Message from the Savior *(John 11:25)*
   I. His Great Proclamation
     ("I am the resurrection and the life")
  II. His Great Clarification
     (That death is not the end of life)
 III. His Great Confirmation
     (Assurance of salvation for all believers)

Heaven: Present and Future *(John 14:1-3)*
   I. The "Mansions" Which "Are" (v. 2*a*)
  II. The "Place" Being "Prepared" (v. 2*b*)
 III. "There" Is Where the Saved Shall "Be" (v. 3)

Heaven *(John 14:1-6)*
   I. Peace (v. 1)
     (Fearlessness)
  II. Promise (vv. 2-3)
     (Security)
 III. Panorama (v. 4)
     (A complete unfolding)
 IV. Paragon (v. 6)
     (The standard of excellence)

Facing Death *(John 14:1-6)*
   I. To the saved. Note the words of comfort.
   (With Christ, vv. 3-4)
  II. To the unsaved. Note the words of instruction.
   (The way of salvation, v. 6)

III. To the wise. Note the words of future hope.
(No room for doubt, v. 2)

Going to Heaven *(John 14:1-6)*
   I. We shall go to a prepared place (v. 2).
     ("I go to prepare a place for you")
  II. We shall go to a precious person (v. 3).
     ("I will . . . receive you unto myself")
 III. We shall go with perfect peace wrought by faith
     (v. 1).
     ("Let not your heart be troubled: . . . believe")
 IV. We shall arrive by way of a plain path (v. 6).
     ("I am the way, the truth, and the life")
  V. We shall be the recipients of profound purpose (v. 3).
     ("There ye may be also")

A Great Verse in Perspective *(John 14:6)*
   I. The Knowing
     ("I am the truth")
  II. The Living
     ("I am the life")
 III. The Going
     ("I am the way")

Greatest Text on the Work of the Church *(John 14:12-14)*
   I. The church's Preparation is through faith (v. 12).
     ("He that believeth")
  II. The church's Prerogative is to do the main
     "work"—Evangelism (v. 12).
     ("The works that I do shall he do also")

40

III. The church's Privilege is to extend Christ's mission into the whole world (v. 12).
("Greater works")
IV. The church's Power must be through the Holy Spirit (v. 12).
("Because I go unto my Father")
V. The church's Program must be built upon Prayer (vv. 13-14).

Answered Prayer *(John 14:13)*
  I. The WAY of Answered Prayer.
("Whatsoever ye shall ask in my name")
 II. The PROMISE of Answered Prayer.
("That will I do")
III. The REASON for Answered Prayer.
("That the Father may be glorified in the Son")

Obedience *(John 14:21)*
  I. Obedience is the mark of true love.
 II. Obedience begats true love.
III. Obedience is rewarded with greater love and enlightenment.

Spiritual Hatred *(John 15:23)*
  I. The fact of spiritual hatred
("He that hateth me")
 II. The object of spiritual hatred
("Hateth me")
III. The far-reaching effects of spiritual hatred
("Hateth my Father also")

Promised Provision *(John 16:24)*
  I. Consider the negative reaction stated.
     ("Nothing")
  II. Consider the positive response called for.
     ("Ask")
  III. Consider the positive results promised.
     ("Ye shall receive")

God's Three-Point Spiritual Program *(John 17:3)*
  I. Provision
     ("Life eternal")
  II. Perception
     ("Know")
  III. Persons
     ("The only true God, and Jesus Christ")

Commissioned Disciples *(John 20:19-21)*
  I. The Salutation—v. 19 (Peaceful Presence)
  II. The Showing—v. 20*a* (Prevailing Proof)
  III. The Seeing—v. 20*b* (Perfect Perception)
  IV. The Sending—v. 21 (Profound Pronouncement)

The Innumerable Works of Christ *(John 20:30-31)*
  I. The Limitless Supply of Christ
  II. The Limitless Power of Christ
  III. The Limited Ability of Man to Comprehend the
     Fullness of Christ
     (We can only believe—this is true faith.)

ACTS

The Issues at Hand *(Acts 1:1-8)*
   I. The "Infallible Proofs" (v. 3)
     A. The empty tomb
     B. The appearances of Christ
  II. The Instructions Given (vv. 4-5)
     A. Don't rely upon human power.
     B. Wait for spiritual power.
 III. The Interlude Explained (vv. 6-8)
     A. Prophetic kingdom of Israel to come later
     B. Power now for witnessing to the world

Pentecost *(Acts 2:1-41)*
   I. A Promise Fulfilled
    (Witness of the Spirit to Israel, vv. 5-11)
  II. A Preacher's Forthrightness
    (Witness of Peter to Israel, vv. 14-36)
 III. A People's Faith
    (Witness of converted Israelites, vv. 37-41)
 IV. A Pattern Furnished
    (Witness of early Christians within the church, vv.
     42-47)

A Paramount Plan *(Acts 4:12)*
   I. It Is an Exclusive Plan
  II. It Is an Exalted Plan
 III. It Is an Exact Plan

Commendable Servitude *(Acts 5:29)*
  I. Superior Dedication
  II. Sacrificial Witness
  III. Submissive Duty
  IV. Superb Evaluation

Victory Amid Church Problems *(Acts 6:1-7)*
  I. The Perplexity of Dissension (v. 1)
    A. Growth without guidance leads to dissension.
    B. Neglect of needy members brings contempt.
  II. The Priority of Disposition (vv. 2-4)
    A. Ministers to minister the Word
    B. Lay leaders to serve the people
  III. The Pleasing Results of Decisiveness (vv. 5-7)
    A. Determination to correct inner problems of the church
    B. Decision to implement organization into church administration
    C. Direct outcome (harmony and growth)

Victory Through Tragedy *(Acts 7:54 to 8:4)*
  I. The Pinpointing
    (Stephen revealed the seriousness of the people's sins.)
  II. The Disowning
    (The people, through their actions, disowned their guilt.)
  III. The Groaning
    (The people could not escape the conviction of guilt produced by Stephen's preaching.)
  IV. The Stoning

(The messenger's death was the beginning of persecution used of God for the spreading of the gospel.)

A Holy Spirit Happening *(Acts 10:1-48)*
I. A heathen proselyte seeks help (vv. 1-8)
II. A hungry apostle commissioned to help the heathen proselyte (vv. 9-16)
III. A heavenly visitation seals a divine transaction (vv. 24-48)

Tribulation and Triumph *(Acts 11:19-26)*
I. The Planting (v. 19)
II. The Progression (vv. 20-21)
III. The Persuasion (vv. 22-24)
IV. The Pattern (vv. 25-26)
    A. Teaching
    B. Testimony ("Called Christians")

Conflict and Progress in the Church *(Acts 12:1-24)*
I. The Slaying (v. 2)
II. The Praying (vv. 5,12)
III. The Delaying (v. 15)
    (Those at the prayer meeting hesitated to believe that their prayers had been answered.)
IV. The Decaying (v. 23)
    (The blasphemous Herod, who had stood in the way of God's work, finally went too far.)
V. The Conveying (v. 24)
    ("The Word of God grew and multiplied.")

The Price and Privilege of Obedience *(Acts 14:8-22)*
   I. Miracle (vv. 8-10)
  II. Misunderstanding (vv. 11-18)
 III. Mugging (v. 19)
  IV. Mystery (v. 20)
   V. Ministering (vv. 21-22)

The True Spirit of Missions *(Acts 16:11-15)*
   I. This was a place with no established worship center (v. 12).

   ("Abiding certain days" indicates no place to assemble.)
  II. This was a place with no established teaching center (v. 12).
 III. This was a place with no established prayer center (v. 13).
  IV. This was a place of hungry hearts (v. 14).
   V. This was a place of responding hearts (v. 15).

Felix, Example of Sinners *(Acts 24:22-25)*
   I. Felix, like *some* sinners, had a "more perfect knowledge" of the truth.
  II. Felix, like *all* sinners, came to the crossroads of decision.
 III. Felix, like *many* sinners, turned away the messenger and the message of God.
  IV. Felix, like *multitudes* of sinners, never again found a "convenient season" for hearing and believing the Word of God.

ROMANS

The Call to Witness *(Rom. 1:16-17)*
   I. We are called to a *bold* witness.
  II. We are called to a *powerful* witness.
 III. We are called to an *unprejudiced* witness.
 IV. We are called to a *sound* witness.

Justification *(Rom. 3:21 to 5:11)*
   I. Its Source—Grace (3:24)
  II. Its Grounds—Blood of Christ (5:9)
 III. Its Means—Faith (5:1)
 IV. Its Evidence—Works (5:1-5)
     (See also Jas. 2:14)

Our Great Gift *(Rom. 5:1-2)*
   I. Our Great Position
    ("Justified by faith")
  II. Our Great Possession
     ("Peace with God")
 III. Our Great Provider
     ("Through our Lord Jesus Christ")
 IV. Our Great Privilege
    ("Access by faith into this grace")

Justification, An Open Door *(Rom. 5:1-5)*
   I. An Open Door to "Peace" (v. 1)
  II. An Open Door to "Grace" (v. 2*a*)
 III. An Open Door to Joy—"Rejoice" (v. 2*b*)
 IV. An Open Door to "Glory" (v. 3)

V. An Open Door to Perseverance (v. 5*a*)
   ("Because the love of God is shed abroad in our
      hearts")
VI. An Open Door to Power (v. 5*b*)
   ("By the Holy Ghost which is given unto us")

Why Christ Died *(Rom. 5:6)*
I. To Meet a Compelling Need
II. To Complete a Marvelous Plan
III. To Mandate a Comforting Revelation

Original Sin, the Great Degradation *(Rom. 5:12)*
I. Death was not in the original plan of God for man.
II. Man's disobedient will produced original sin.
III. The original creation of God, in its entirety, has
   fallen under the curse of death through original sin.
IV. Original sin, the great degradation, is annulled
   only by justification through Jesus Christ (See
   5:15-19).

Salvation's Application *(Rom. 6:8)*
I. Here salvation is presented as a past event.
II. Here salvation is proclaimed as a present pos-
   session.
III. Here salvation is perceived as a future hope.

A Worthwhile Observation *(Rom. 6:16)*
I. Consider the Searching Question.

II. Consider the Subject of Concern.
III. Consider the Serious Deduction.

The Spirit's Message to the Christian *(Rom. 8:14-16)*
I. The Spirit's inner work makes us aware of our salvation (v. 14).
II. The Spirit's watchcare over us seals our adoption unto salvation (v. 15).
III. The Spirit's witness to us gives us the assurance of our security.

Being an Overcomer *(Rom. 8:18)*
I. Reasoning *Versus* Depression
II. Glory *Versus* Suffering
III. Revelation *Versus* Present Circumstances

God's Goodness *(Rom. 8:28)*
I. God designs good for mankind.
II. God demands that proper conditions be met in order to claim his goodness.
III. God denounces the power of any force to hold back his best interests in behalf of his faithful servants.

War and Victory *(Rom. 8:36-37)*
I. Our Continual Challenge
("We are killed all the day long.")
II. Our Continual Foe
("We are accounted as sheep for the slaughter.")

III. Our Continual Victory
("Nay, in all these things we are more than conquerors through him that loved us.")

The Greatness of God's Love *(Rom. 8:38-39)*
I. The Profound Indescribability of God's Love
II. The Pronounced Indestructibility of God's Love
III. The Possessed Inseparability of God's Love

The New Dimension *(Rom. 10:9-11)*
I. The Dimension of Faith.
II. The Dimension of Power.
III. The Dimension of Divine Approval.

Grounds for Total Commitment *(Rom. 12:1)*
I. Affectionate Consideration
("I beseech you . . . by the mercies of God")
II. Acceptable Expediency
("Acceptable unto God")
III. Agreeable Participation
("Which is your reasonable service")

Dedication, Why? *(Rom. 12:1)*
I. Revelation—Dedication is God's will.
II. Reason—God's gift of salvation concludes that dedication is an expected response.
III. Reflection—Reflection upon God's grace teaches that dedication is the only way of fulfilling his will in our lives.

Spiritual Gifts and Attitudes *(Rom. 12:1 to 15:3)*

I. Attitudes relative to those inside the church (12:9-16)

II. Attitudes relative to those outside the church (12:17-21)

III. Attitudes relative to citizenship (13:1-10)

IV. Attitudes relative to the weaker brethren (13:14; 15:3)

An Analogy for the Church *(Rom. 12:4-8)*
(Text—v. 5)

I. The analogy shows that no individual member of Christ's body can function effectively alone.

II. The analogy shows that no individual member of Christ's body is superior in function to any other member of his body.

III. The analogy shows that all members of Christ's body must work in unison to prevent hindrance to the cause of Christ.

Winning Characteristics of Christians *(Rom. 12:8-18)*

I. Simplicity (v. 8)

II. Diligence (v. 8)

III. Cheerfulness (v. 8)

IV. Loving (v. 9)

V. Kindness (v. 10)

VI. Fervent (v. 11)

VII. Patience (v. 12)

VIII. Peaceable (v. 18)

Three Dynamics That Win *(Rom. 12:9)*
   I. The Dynamic of Perfect Love
   II. The Dynamic of Proper Abstinence
   III. The Dynamic of Profound Good

The Christian and Vengeance *(Rom. 12:19-21)*
   I. The Commandment (v. 19)
      A. "Avenge not yourselves."
      B. "Give place unto wrath."
      C. Recognize God's wisdom in relation to vengeance.
   II. The Supplication (vv. 20-21)
      A. Exercise Christian benevolence toward the enemy.
      B. Acknowledge the power of God over evil.
      C. Trust in God to keep his word in relation to vengeance.

The Diligent Christian *(Rom. 13:11-14)*
   I. His diligence is demonstrated through awareness.
      A. He knows (v. 11*a*).
      B. He awakes (v. 11*b*).
   II. His diligence is demonstrated through action.
      A. He casts off (v. 12*a*).
      B. He walks (v. 13).
   III. His diligence is demonstrated through apparel.
      A. He puts on light (v. 12*b*).
      B. He puts on Christ (v. 14).

Putting on Christ *(Rom. 13:12-14)*
- I. In Our Dress (v. 12)
- II. In Our Walk (v. 13)
- III. In Our Maintenance (v. 14)

Consider the Christian *(Rom. 15:13)*
- I. His Present State
  ("Filled with all joy and peace")
- II. His Ongoing Outlook
  ("That [they might] abound in hope")
- III. His Source of Power
  ("Power of the Holy Ghost")

1 CORINTHIANS

The Preaching of the Cross *(1 Cor. 1:17-18)*
    I. Some are called to preach the cross.
   II. Many curse and condemn the preaching of the cross.
  III. Some come to Christ through the preaching of the cross.
  IV. Many never find the power of the cross because of preaching that substitutes ceremonialism (v. 17).

Looking Ahead *(1 Cor. 2:9)*
    I. Faith looks beyond temporal vision.
    ("Eye hath not seen")
   II. Faith goes beyond uncertain sounds.
   ("Nor hath ear heard")
  III. Faith reaches beyond human emotions.
  ("Neither have entered into the heart of man")
  IV. Faith rises above human expectation.
  ("The things which God hath prepared for them that love him")

Spiritual Separation *(1 Cor. 2:14)*
    I. The *condition* of the natural man separates him from spiritual truth.
   II. The *callousness* of the natural man separates him from spiritual truth.
  III. The *cynicism* of the natural man separates him from spiritual truth.

IV. The *carnality* of the natural man separates him from spiritual truth.

Carnality in the Church *(1 Cor. 3:1-4,9)*
I. Its Cause
   (Lack of spiritual growth)
II. Its Course
   (Weakness and nonproficiency)
III. Its Curse
   (Church division)
IV. Its Cure
   (Acknowledge servitude of all under God)

Ministers of Christ *(1 Cor. 4:1-4)*
I. Here our attention is *Affixed* upon the respect due the ministers of Christ.
II. Here we find that faithfulness to duty *Approves* the ministers of Christ worthy of respect.
III. Here we learn that the *Actions* of His ministers can only be judged by Christ.

Obedience *(1 Cor. 4:2)*
I. To be obedient we must grasp its meaning.
II. To be obedient we must follow our example. (Christ)
III. To be obedient we must feel the need of it. (desire)
IV. To be obedient we must respect the fact that it is a command.

The Temple of the Holy Ghost *(1 Cor. 6:19-20)*

    I. It Should Be a Holy Place.
       ("Of the Holy Ghost")
   II. It Should Be a Happy Place.
       ("Which ye have of God")
 III. It Should Be a Harmonious Place.
       ("Ye are not your own")
 IV. It Should Be a Healthy Place.
       ("In your body")
  V. It Should Be an Honorable Place.
       ("Therefore glorify God")
 VI. It Should Be a Humble Place.
       ("Your body and . . . your spirit . . . are God's")

Lessons for Ransomed Souls *(1 Cor. 6:19-20)*

    I. The highest price
       ("Ye are bought with a price")
  II. The humbling revelation
       ("Ye are not your own")
 III. The halting conclusion
       ("Therefore glorify God")

The Christian Race *(1 Cor. 9:24-25)*

    I. Duty's Call
  II. Designated Course
 III. Disciplined Contention
 IV. Divine Concession

Temptation's Limitations *(1 Cor. 10:13)*

I. Temptation may take us, but it need not overtake us.

II. Temptation may be common, but it need not be compromised.

III. Temptation may be powerful, but it is not all-powerful.

The Gospel Which Paul Preached *(1 Cor. 15:1-8)*

I. It was the gospel which he preached consistently (v. 1*a*).

II. It was the gospel which he preached convincingly (vv. 1*b*-2*a*).

III. It was the gospel which he preached by confirmation (vv. 3-8).

Empty Things on Easter *(1 Cor. 15:3-8,12,17)*

I. There is the empty cross.

II. There is the empty tomb.

III. There are the empty doubts of unbelievers.

The Negative Approach to the Doctrine of the Resurrection *(1 Cor. 15:12-18)*

I. Insane (Absurdity)—To deny the resurrection in light of the proof of Christ's resurrection (vv. 12-13).

II. In vain—To deny the resurrection denies all hope of life after death (vv. 14,17).

III. Profane—To deny the resurrection of Christ, and thus of the dead in Christ, is to denounce all preachers of the gospel as false witnesses (v. 15).

IV. Disdain—To deny life after death to those who die in Christ is to reach the ultimate in contempt for the doctrine of the resurrection (v. 18).

The Great Withholders *(1 Cor. 15:51-55)*

I. Corruption withholds from God's presence (v. 53a).

II. Mortality withholds from God's presence (v. 53b).

III. God has provided for the removal of these great withholders (vv. 51-52).
   A. Possible translation
   B. Positive resurrection

IV. God even issues a challenge against these great withholders (vv. 54-55).

A Call to Faithfulness *(1 Cor. 15:58)*

I. Paul Calls for Reflection.
   ("Therefore")

II. Paul Calls for Reaction.
   ("Steadfast, unmoveable . . . abounding")

III. Paul Calls for Reliance.
   ("Forasmuch as ye know")

2 CORINTHIANS

A Threefold Test of Integrity *(2 Cor. 1:12-15)*
  I. The Testimony of Conscience (v. 12a)
  II. The Testimony of Conversation (v. 12b)
  III. The Testimony of Confidence (vv. 13-15)

Christian Love *Versus* Satanic Opportunity *(2 Cor. 2:1-11)*
  I. Love Confirmed by Forgiveness
  II. Love Conveyed Through the "Person of Christ"
  III. Love Cautions Against Satan's Devices
    (By using an unforgiving attitude, Satan can scandalize the ministry and the church.)

Christian Triumph *(2 Cor. 2:14-17)*
  I. The Christian's triumph is Christ (v. 14).
  II. The Christian's triumph is expressed in service to Christ (vv. 15-16).
  III. The measure of the Christian's triumph is his fidelity (v. 17).

The Disease of Spiritual Blindness *(2 Cor. 4:3-4)*
  I. It is a common disease.
    A. The symptom of worldliness
    B. The symptom of an easy conscience about sinning
    C. The symptom of continued rejection of the gospel invitation
  II. It is a Satan-induced disease.

A. Sinners are the product of satanic deception.
B. Sinners are victims of satanic persuasion.
III. It is a disease which must be dealt with spiritually.
A. The blindness of sinners results from spiritual darkness which veils the light of the gospel.
B. Faith in Christ alone can remove the veil of darkness and bring spiritual healing.

The State of the Ungodly *(2 Cor. 4:3-4)*
I. They are lost (v. 3).
A. The hiding of the gospel is related to their spiritual need.
B. Thus the hiding of the gospel renders it ineffectual for them.
II. They are blind (v. 4a).
A. They are held under the curse of satanic influence.
("The god of this world")
B. Their blind condition is a witness to the cause for their spiritual blindness.
III. They are in total darkness (v. 4b).
A. Even blind persons can learn and find ways to overcome their darkness.
B. But those who willfully reject Christ are rebelling against the only source of light which can deliver them from their darkness.

An Encouraging Lesson for All Christians *(2 Cor. 4:8-11)*
I. We can face trouble without *distress* (v. 8a).

II. We can face perplexity without *despair* (v. 8*b*).

III. We can face persecution without *disassociation* (v. 9*a*).

IV. We can face dejection without *disaster* (v. 9*b*).

V. We can face death with *delight* (vv. 10-11).

A Scriptural Affidavit for Christians *(2 Cor. 5:1-11)*
I. Assurance ("We know," v. 1*a*)
II. Anticipation ("We have," v. 1*b*)
III. Anxiousness ("We groan," v. 2)
IV. Abrogation ("We shall not," v. 3)
V. Affirmation ("We are," vv. 6-8)
VI. Accountability ("We must," v. 10)
VII. Advocation ("We persuade," v. 11)

Christians at the Judgment Seat *(2 Cor. 5:10)*
I. There is the *judicial* aspect of the judgment.
II. There is the *accountability* aspect of the judgment.
III. There is the *profit or loss* aspect of the judgment.

Judgment of Believers *(2 Cor. 5:10)*
I. Who will appear?
("All" Christians)
II. Where will we appear?
("Before the judgment seat of Christ")
III. Why must we appear?
(To "receive" judgment)
IV. What may we expect?
(Just judgment "according to that he hath done")

Conversion and Commission *(2 Cor. 5:17-20)*
  I. The Great Charge—SALVATION (v. 17)
  II. The Grace Commended—SOURCE (vv. 18-19*a*)
  III. The Glorious Commitment—SERVICE (vv. 19*b*-20)

The Gospel Which Paul Ministered *(2 Cor. 6:1-10)*
  I. The gospel which is sufficient (v. 1)
  II. The gospel which must be accepted in the time of opportunity (v. 2)
  III. The gospel which must be preached and accepted in an unoffensive way (vv. 3-4*a*)
  IV. The gospel which calls for sacrificial service (vv. 4*b*-10)

Three Great Contrasts Between the Gospel and the World *(2 Cor. 6:14-18)*
  I. The Contrast of Saints and Sinners (v. 14)
    A. Righteousness breaks fellowship with unrighteousness.
    B. Spiritual enlightenment breaks communion with spiritual darkness.
  II. The Contrast of Christianity and Idolatry (vv. 15*a*-16*a*)
    A. There can be no harmony (concord) between the two.
    B. There can be no spiritual connection (the temple of God) between the two.
  III. The Contrast of Believers and Atheists (v. 15*b*)
    A. Believers are "the temple of the living God."
    B. Atheists deny the very existence of God.

Some Exhortations Worth Considering *(2 Cor. 7:1-11)*
I. Exhortation to grow in holiness (v. 1)
II. Exhortation to give due respect to the ministers of the gospel (v. 2)
III. Exhortation to be sorry for sin (recognition of guilt, vv. 8-10)
IV. Exhortation to approve ourselves through repentance (v. 11)

Godward Charity *(2 Cor. 9:6-7)*
I. God blesses the bountiful giver (v. 6).
II. God blesses the deliberate giver (v. 7*a*).
III. God blesses the cheerful giver (v. 7*b*).

Godward Benevolence *(2 Cor. 9:7)*
I. Godward benevolence should come from a predetermined arrangement.
II. Godward benevolence must be accomplished by a proper attitude.
III. Godward benevolence will beget God's approval.

Saints and Suffering (Paul's Example) *(2 Cor. 12:7-10)*
I. The "thorn" was "given."
  A. Allowed of God
  B. Messenger of Satan
II. The "thorn" had a purpose.
  A. "Lest I should be exalted above measure"
  B. "I besought the Lord . . . that it might depart"
III. The "thorn" provided an occasion for greater blessings.

A. "My grace is sufficient for thee."
B. "My strength is made perfect in weakness."

Rewarding Frustration *(2 Cor. 12:7,10)*
    I. Deleted Exaltation
      ("Lest I should be exalted above measure")
   II. Abundant Revelation
      ("Through the abundance of the revelations")
  III. Unexpected Transformation
      ("For when I am weak, then am I strong")

GALATIANS

Galatian Folly *(Gal. 1:1-12)*
   I. Their Position (v. 6*b*)
      ("Called you into the grace of Christ")
   II. Their Problem (v. 6*a*)
      ("So soon removed")
   III. Their Perversion (vv. 6*c*-7)
      ("Another gospel: Which is not another")
   IV. Their Provision (vv. 11-12)
      ("The gospel which was preached of me . . . the revelation of Jesus Christ.")

The Triumphant Partnership *(Gal. 2:20)*
   I. The Christian is allied with Christ in death.
   II. The Christian is allied with Christ in life.
   III. The Christian is allied with Christ in total victory.

Digression from Dedication *(Gal. 3:1-5)*
   I. Their Disappointment to Paul (v. 1)
      ("O foolish Galatians")
   II. Their Disenchantment with the Doctrine of Grace (v. 1)
      ("Who hath bewitched you?")
   III. Their Disobedience to the Truth (v. 1)
      ("That ye should not obey the truth")
   IV. Their Diversion from the Work of the Holy Spirit (v. 2)
      ("Received ye the Spirit by the works of the law, or by the hearing of faith?")

A Scriptural Conclusion *(Gal. 3:22)*
   I. This Scripture points out mankind's *depravity.*
   II. This Scripture points to mankind's possibility of *deliverance.*
   III. This Scripture pinpoints mankind's *deliverer.*

Confusion About Cleansing *(Gal. 4:8-11)*
   I. Paul reminded the Galatian Christians of what they had been (v. 8).
   ("Ye knew not God.")
   II. Paul reminded the Galatian Christians of what they had become (v. 9*a*).
   ("Ye have known God.")
   III. Paul warned the Galatian Christians against the error they were making (v. 9*b*).
   ("Ye desire again to be in bondage?")

A Holy Expectation *(Gal. 5:25)*
   I. It is based upon an assumption.
   ("If")
   II. It is based upon an awareness.
   ("Live in the Spirit")
   III. It is based upon an action.
   ("Walk in the Spirit")

Benevolent Attitudes *(Gal. 6:1-3)*
   I. It is a message both for the weak and the strong.
   II. It is a message directed primarily to those strong in the faith.
   III. It is a message prohibiting judgment of other Christians.

IV. It is a message which, when properly applied, will
     bring praise to God.
     (See Rom. 15:17.)

A Pattern for Restoration *(Gal. 6:1-4)*
   I. "Restore" in an attitude of meekness (v. 1).
  II. "Bear" each other's burdens in love (v. 2).
 III. "Prove" own works instead of judging others (v. 4).

EPHESIANS

The Blood of Christ *(Eph. 1:7)*

   I. The blood of Christ has *called* us back from sin's curse.

  II. The blood of Christ has *covered* our guilt before God.

 III. The blood of Christ has *crowned* us with the riches of grace.

Salvation and Security *(Eph. 1:13-14)*

    I. The Source
("In whom ye also trusted")

   II. The Substance
("Your salvation")

  III. The Sealing
("Sealed with that holy Spirit of promise")

 IV. The Surety
("Which is the earnest of our inheritance")

Commendable Christian Goals *(Eph. 1:17-19)*

   I. A deeper knowledge of God
("May give unto you the spirit of wisdom and revelation in the knowledge of him")

  II. A continued spiritual enlightenment
("The eyes of your understanding being enlightened")

 III. A desire to enlarge the hope of our calling
("That ye may know what is the hope of his calling")

 IV. A greater appreciation for our position

("The riches of the glory of his inheritance in the saints")
V. A special awareness of the power manifested within us
("What is the exceeding greatness of his power to us-ward who believe")

God's Description of the Unregenerate *(Eph. 2:1-3)*
I. Their Position (v. 1)
("Dead in trespasses and sins")
II. Their Performance (v. 2)
A. Walking in accord with Satan's dictates
B. Walking in disobedience to God
III. Their Perversion (v. 3*a*)
("Fulfilling the desires of the flesh and of the mind")
IV. Their Predicament (v. 3*b*)
("By nature the children of wrath")

Prescription for Salvation and Discipleship *(Eph. 2:8-10)*
I. God's Grace—Man's Faith
II. God's Gift—Not Man's Works
III. God's Glory—Not Man's Boastfulness
IV. God's Works—Man's Obedience

Our Future and God's Will *(Eph. 2:10)*
I. In Christ we have relinquished the right to plan our own future.
II. God alone knows how best to direct our future for the fulfilling of his purpose.

III. Christ will lead us into God's perfect will as we surrender to his call

Significant Thoughts from a Great Man's Prayer *(Eph. 3:16-19)*
   I. Strength (v. 16)
   II. Security (v. 17)
   III. Scrutiny (v. 18)
   IV. Sanctification (v. 19)

Unity's Reward *(Eph. 4:1-16)*
   I. The Plan (v. 2)
   II. The Provision (v. 3)
   III. The Perspective (vv. 4-7)
   IV. The Perfecting (vv. 11-16)

Some Positive Negatives of Christianity *(Eph. 4:17-32)*
   I. "Walk not" (v. 17).
   II. "Put off" (v. 22).
   III. "Put away" (vv. 25,31).
   IV. "Let not" (vv. 26,29).
   V. "Grieve not" (v. 30).

Life: Past and Present *(Eph. 5:1-21)*
   I. Departure from the past life of sinfulness (vv. 1-7)
   II. Determination to live the fruitful life (vv. 9-20)
   III. Dedication to the congenial life (v. 21)

A Command for Children *(Eph. 6:1-3)*

   I. The Response It Requires (v. 1*a*)
      "Obey"
  II. The Reasonableness of It (v. 1*b*)
      "For this is right"
 III. The Reward It Promises (vv. 2-3)
    A. "Commandment with promise" (v. 2)
    B. "It may be well with thee" (v. 3)

PHILIPPIANS

Thankfulness for Others *(Phil. 1:3-6)*
I. Thankfulness for fond memories (v. 3)
II. Thankfulness expressed through prayer (v. 4)
III. Thankfulness for brotherly fellowship (v. 5)
IV. Thankfulness for the confidence we share (v. 6)

Divine Inducement to Christian Duty *(Phil. 1:9-11)*
I. The Abounding Love Requested (v. 9)
   A. Here is the basis of benevolent knowledge.
   B. Here is the basis of benevolent judgment.
II. The Approved Law Recited (v. 10)
   A. The law of Christ is truth most excellent.
   B. The actions of believers express their approval of Christ's law.
      1. Our sincerity reveals truth.
      2. Our unoffensiveness reveals truth.
III. The Applied Lesson Revealed (v. 11)
   A. It results in personal righteousness.
   B. It results in glory and praise to God.

A Life or Death Commitment *(Phil. 1:21)*
("For to me to live is Christ")
   I. A Conscientious Commitment
   II. A Commendable Commitment
("And to die is gain")
   I. A Confident Commitment
   II. A Comforting Commitment

How Death Becomes Gain *(Phil. 1:21)*

    I. In death we gain release from the burdens of a physical body.

   II. In death we gain release from the burdens of a material body.

  III. In death we gain release from the presence of sin.

  IV. In death we gain the eternal presence of Christ.

   V. In death we gain the eternal presence of saints of all ages.

The Comforting Confidence *(Phil. 1:21-26)*

    I. Ready in Life (v. 21*a*)

  II. Ready in Death (v. 21*b*)

  III. Ready in Divine Providence (vv. 22-26)

Credible Works *(Phil. 2:12-13)*

    I. It is not "work *for* your salvation."

      A. Salvation by works is not suggested in this text.

      B. Neither does this text imply that a Christian cannot remain saved unless he works.

  II. It is "work out your salvation."

      A. The emphasis is upon working out what one already has.

      B. There has to be a crop before the farmer can work it out.

  III. It is God who has done the initial work.

      A. "For it is God which worketh in you both to will and to do his good pleasure."

      B. We show the work of God within as we work out a credible evidence of salvation for the world to see.

Victory Over Anxiety *(Phil. 4:6-7)*
I. Acknowledge the Problem—Worry.
II. Absorb the Plan—Prayer.
III. Accept the Provision—Peace.

Powerful Prescription for Liberty *(Phil. 4:7)*
I. Person—"God"
II. Possession—"Peace"
III. Power—"Passeth All Understanding"
IV. Presence—"Christ Jesus"

The God Paul Proclaimed *(Phil. 4:19)*
I. Paul Proclaimed a Personal God.
("My God")
II. Paul Proclaimed a Positive God.
("Shall")
III. Paul Proclaimed a Providing God.
("Supply all your need")
IV. Paul Proclaimed a Plenteous God.
("According to his riches")
V. Paul Proclaimed a Piteous God.
("By Christ Jesus")

COLOSSIANS

Our Inherited Fellowship *(Col. 1:12-14)*
I. We are brought into the fellowship of God.
II. We are brought into the fellowship of the saints.
III. We are brought into the fellowship of light.
IV. We are brought into the fellowship of forgiveness.
V. We are brought into the fellowship of these things through the blood of Christ.

The Call to Loftiness *(Col. 3:1-4)*
I. The Grounds of the Call
    A. "Ye [are] risen with Christ" (v. 1).
    B. "Your life is hid with Christ in God" (v. 3).
    C. "Ye shall also appear with him in glory" (v. 4).
II. The Means of Fulfilling the Call
    A. "Seek those things which are above" (v. 1).
    B. "Set your affection on things above" (v. 2).

Speaking Wisely *(Col. 4:6)*
I. Our speech should be caring, but powerful. ("With grace")
II. Our speech should be kind ("seasoned"), but positive ("with salt")
Salt is a preservative and denotes stability.
III. Our speech should be sharing, but purposeful. ("How ye ought to answer every man")

1 THESSALONIANS

A Supreme Example *(1 Thess. 1:3-4)*
   I. In Faith
      ("Your work of faith")
  II. In Love
      ("And labour of love")
 III. In Patience
      ("And patience of hope")
  IV. In Assurance
      ("Knowing . . . your election of God")

Basis of Our Present Hope *(1 Thess. 1:10)*
   I. The Doctrine of Justification
      ("Jesus, which delivered us from the wrath to come")
  II. The Doctrine of the Resurrection of Christ
      ("Whom he raised from the dead, even Jesus")
 III. The Doctrine of the Second Coming of Christ
      ("And to wait for his Son from heaven")

Paul's Fruitful Ministry *(1 Thess. 2:1-13)*
Text (v. 1), "Our [ministry] in unto you, that it was not in vain"
(Paul is really saying "our ministry unto you was not fruitless.")
His ministry was fruitful for several reasons:
   I. Preached the Gospel with Boldness (v. 2)
  II. Preached True Doctrine (v. 3)
 III. Was a Good Steward of the Gospel (vv. 4-7)

IV. Loved Their Souls (v. 8)
V. Was Industrious (v. 9)
VI. Was an Example (v. 10)
VII. Gave Instructions in Holiness (vv. 11-12)
VIII. They Received the Word (v. 13)

A Good Example *(1 Thess. 2:10)*
I. A good example is approved before other believers.
II. A good example is approved before God.
III. A good example is approved through proper behavior.

Our Great Crowning Day *(1 Thess. 4:13-18)*
I. The Great Announcement (vv. 13-14)
II. The Great Appearing (v. 16*a*)
III. The Great Arising (v. 16*b*)
IV. The Great Arrival (v. 17*a*)
V. The Great Attainment (v. 17*b*)
VI. The Great Acclamation (v. 18)

Our Divine Appointment *(1 Thess. 5:9-10)*
I. What God has not appointed us unto (v. 9*a*)
II. What God has appointed us unto (v. 9*b*)
III. What the assurance is which the appointment brings unto us (v. 10)

A Question of Abstinence *(1 Thess. 5:22)*

I. The statement should be considered as a command.

II. The statement calls upon individuals to make a choice.

III. The statement suggests a consequence for compromise.

(The "appearance of evil," if compromised, can lead to sin and suffering.)

2 THESSALONIANS

Facing Present Trouble *(2 Thess. 1:7-10)*
  I. Our present trouble is overshadowed by our future victory in the coming day of the Lord.
  II. Our present seeming defeat at the hands of ungodly troublemakers is overshadowed by the just judgment in the coming day of the Lord.
  III. Our present circumstances in troublesome times are overshadowed by the glory our faithfulness shall bring to Christ in the coming day of the Lord.

Faithfulness and Rewards *(2 Thess. 1:3-6)*
  I. Faithfulness
    A. Growing faith (v. 3*a*)
    B. Patient faith (v. 4*a*)
    C. Enduring faith (v. 4*b*)
  II. Rewards
    A. Shared love (v. 3*b*)
    B. Manifested love (v. 5)
    C. Recompensing love (v. 6)

Notes on Church Discipline *(2 Thess. 3:6-15)*
(Note: This is a command written to a local church.)
  I. Church discipline reprimands disorderliness (v. 6*a*).
  II. Church discipline must be established upon proper teaching (v. 6*b*).
  III. Church discipline must be established upon proper example (vv. 7-9).

IV. Church discipline must be recognized as being equally binding upon all members (vv. 10-12).
V. Church discipline must be administered in mercy (vv. 13-15).

1 TIMOTHY

Christ, the Great Link *(1 Tim. 2:5)*
- I. Monotheism
- II. Mediator
- III. Mankind

Why the Incarnation? *(1 Tim. 3:16)*
- I. Man was a sinner with no hope of salvation by his own works.
- II. Man was a religious being with no hope of salvation through his own religious efforts.
- III. Man needed a pure object of worship which could interpose in his behalf.
- IV. Only the Son of God in flesh could become the acceptable mediator for mankind.

Four Marks of Apostasy *(1 Tim. 4:1-2)*
- I. Cardinal Separation (v. 1*a*)
  ("Some shall depart from the faith")
- II. Corrupting Spirits (v. 1*b*)
  ("Giving heed to seducing spirits")
- III. Calamitous Speaking (v. 2*a*)
  ("Speaking lies in hypocrisy")
- IV. Callous Searing (v. 2*b*)
  ("Conscience seared with a hot iron")

A Lesson for Christian Youth *(1 Tim. 4:12)*

I. Here is a warning against possible youthful offenses.

II. Here is an exhortation to commendable conduct.

III. Here is a formula for developing qualities that demand respect.

2 TIMOTHY

The God-Given Spirit *(2 Tim. 1:7)*
    I. A Spirit That Keeps Us from Fear
    II. A Spirit That Produces Power
    III. A Spirit That Generates Love
    IV. A Spirit That Assures Sanity

True Discipleship *(2 Tim. 1:9)*
    I. Called to Salvation
    II. Called to Sanctification
    III. Called to Sound Doctrine
        (Salvation by grace—not works)

A Studious Servant *(2 Tim. 2:15)*
    I. He Is an Approved Servant
    II. He Is an Unashamed Servant
    III. He Is a Sound-teaching Servant

Requirements of Religious Educators *(2 Tim. 2:15)*
    I. Educability.
        ("Study")
    II. Accountability.
        ("Show thyself approved unto God")
    III. Acceptability.
        ("A workman that needed not to be ashamed")
    IV. Capability.
        ("Rightly dividing the word of truth")

Witnessing *(2 Tim. 2:24-26)*
I. Here we have instructions as to the proper approach to witnessing (v. 24).
II. Here we are informed as to the condition of those to whom we witness (v. 25).
III. Here we are inspired to achieve the desired goal of our witnessing (v. 26).

Modern Boasters *(2 Tim. 3:1-4)*
I. Man's self-sufficiency is a boast against his need of God.
II. Man's self-worship is a boast against his need of God.
III. Man's self-knowledge complex is a boast against his need of God.
IV. Man's self-savior obsession is a boast against his need of God.

Facing Persecution *(2 Tim. 3:12)*
I. This verse anticipates a question.
("Yea")
II. This verse gives a profound answer to the anticipated question.
III. This verse calls for supreme dedication to Christ.

Consider the Scriptures *(2 Tim. 3:16-17)*
I. Consider the Source of Scriptural Truth.
II. Consider the Scope of Scriptural Truth.
III. Consider the Solidarity of Scriptural Truth.

Remedy of a Compromising Attitude *(2 Tim. 4:2-4)*
   I. Don't Be a Word-Wrester.
   II. Don't Be a Tickling-Teacher.
   III. Don't Be a Fable-Fibber.

TITUS

Winning Qualities of Good Servants *(Titus 2:7-8)*
    I. A good servant will set a good example in works.
    II. A good servant will set a good example in doctrine.
    III. A good servant will set a good example in speech.

Our Unique Position *(Titus 2:11-14)*
    I. In the Presence of the Gospel of Grace (v. 11)
    II. In the Petition for Godliness Given (v. 12)
    III. In the Prophecy of the Glorious Hope Guaranteed (v. 13)
    IV. In the Privilege of the Good Works Gained (v. 14)

The Great Transaction *(Titus 2:14)*
    I. The Giving
    II. The Redeeming
    III. The Purifying
    IV. The Inspiring

Our Hope of Salvation *(Titus 3:4-6)*
    I. Our hope of salvation is a past accomplishment (v. 4).
    II. Our hope of salvation is not based upon our works (v. 5).
    III. Our hope of salvation is fulfilled in Christ (v. 6).

Witnesses of the Word *(Titus 3:8)*
We are witnesses of the Word by:
   I. Believing It
      ("This is a faithful saying")
  II. ("That thou affirm [it] constantly")
 III. Living It
      ("Careful to maintain good works")

PHILEMON

Three Notable Men *(Philem. 1:1-21)*
   I. Paul (vv. 1,8)
      A. An apostle
      B. A prisoner
      C. A petitioner
  II. Philemon (vv. 1-7)
      A. A beloved man
      B. A believing man
      C. A benevolent man
 III. Onesimus (vv. 10-21)
      A. A runaway slave
      B. A repenting thief
      C. A returning convert
        (From "unprofitable" to "profitable")

Philemon, Man of Practical Life and Faith
(Philem. 5-7)
   I. The Fact Acknowledged (v. 5)
  II. The Effectual Ministry (v. 6)
 III. The Results Generated (v. 7)
      A. Joy
      B. Consolation
      C. Refreshment

Qualities That Demand Confidence *(Philem. 20-21)*
   I. Paul Had Confidence in Philemon's Charity.
  II. Paul Had Confidence in Philemon's Obedience.
 III. Paul Had Confidence in Philemon's Extensibility

HEBREWS

A Question of Escape *(Heb. 2:3)*
  I. This verse should alarm unbelievers who reject Christ.
  II. This verse gives answer to skeptics who deny the inspiration of the Scriptures.
  III. This verse allows for no other plan of salvation apart from the Gospel of Jesus Christ.
  IV. This verse assures that judgment will come, from which many will not escape.

How Do We See Jesus? *(Heb. 2:9)*
  I. We should see him as the Sacred Son who became a servant.
  II. We should see him as the Suffering Servant who became our Savior.
  III. We should see him as the Sacrificial Savior who became our Sanctification.

Flesh and Blood *(Heb. 2:14)*
  I. The Dreadful Perdition upon Flesh and Blood
  II. The Divine Partaker of Flesh and Blood
  III. The Demanded Propitiation for Flesh and Blood
  IV. The Destroyed Power Over Flesh and Blood

The Humility of Christ *(Heb. 2:14-18)*
I. His Condescension from the Higher Order (v. 16).
II. His Compassionate Sacrifice Divinely Ordained (v. 17).
III. His Comforting Ministry in Behalf of Others (v. 18).

Benefits of the Word *(Heb. 4:12)*
I. No heart is helped more than that which *heeds* the Word.
II. No heart is healthier than that which *honors* the Word.
III. No heart is happier than that which *heralds* the Word.

Invitation to the Prayer Throne *(Heb. 4:16)*
I. An Invitation to Decisive Praying
("Let us")
II. An Invitation to Bold Praying
("Come boldly")
III. An Invitation to Expedient Praying
("In time of need")
IV. An Invitation to Effectual Praying
("That we may obtain")

The Sure Thing *(Heb. 7:25)*
I. The Scriptural Statement
("He is able")
II. The Sufficient Salvation
("Save . . . to the uttermost")
III. The Seeking Sinner
("That come unto God by him")

A Powerful Cleansing *(Heb. 7:25)*
I. Power to Pay the PRICE for Sin
II. Power to Purge the POLLUTION of Sin
III. Power to Prevent the PREVALENCE of Sin

Understanding the Fullness of Christ *(Heb. 9:24-28)*
I. Consider the significance of the backward look (vv. 24-26*a*).
II. Consider the significance of the present look (v. 26*b*).
III. Consider the significance of the inward look (v. 27).
IV. Consider the significance of the future look (v. 28).

Faith, Our True Guide *(Heb. 11:1)*
I. Faith is not subjective to immediateness.
II. Faith is not limited to the senses.
III. Faith is not undiscernable, being both substantiated and corroborated.

Faith's Legacy *(Heb. 11:13)*
I. They Died.
- A. Death came because they were the children of Adam in the flesh and under the curse.
- B. They died in faith because they were Abraham's children, having faith like unto his.

II. They Received Not.
- A. They did not receive the promise in a literal sense.
- B. They walked not by sight but by faith.

III. They Confessed.
   A. That this world was not their permanent home.
   B. Their confession of faith lives on as an encouragement for saints of all ages.

Faith's Evidence *(Heb. 11:17-19)*
   I. True Faith Is Proved Through Testing
   II. True Faith Is Proved Through Obedience
   III. True Faith Is Proved Through Worship
   IV. True Faith Is Proved Through Works

JAMES

Overcoming Temptation *(Jas. 1:2-4,12)*
   I. Joy Amid Temptation (v. 2)
  II. Knowledge Amid Temptation (v. 3)
 III. Patience Amid Temptation (v. 4)
 IV. Endurance Amid Temptation (v. 12)

Blueprint for God-Given Wisdom *(Jas. 1:5-7)*
   I. Recognize the Need (v. 5a).
  II. Desire Wisdom (v. 5b).
 III. Meet the Conditions (v. 6).
     ("Ask in faith, nothing wavering")
 IV. Receive on the Basis of Promise (vv. 6-7).

Perfect Religion *(Jas. 1:25-27)*
   I. "Doer" Religion (v. 25)
  II. Tongue Bridled Religion (v. 26)
 III. Benevolent Religion (v. 27a)
 IV. Unspotted Religion (v. 27b)

Three Great Problems of Christians *(Jas. 2:15-17)*
   I. There is the problem of the destitute faced by the Christian (v. 15).
  II. There is the problem of indifference on the part of many Christians (v. 16).
 III. There is the problem of an inactive faith committed by the Christian (v. 17).

Why Our Present Hope Should Be in God *(Jas. 4:14)*
  I. Because of our inability to know the future
      ("Ye know not what shall be on the morrow")
  II. Because of the uncertainty of physical life
      ("What is your life?")
  III. Because of the swiftness of life's span
      ("Appeareth for a little time")

1 PETER

What's Happening? *(1 Pet. 1:1)*
   I. What's in a Name?
      A. "Peter"
      B. Means "The Rock"
      C. An apostle—God's messenger
   II. What's in a Title?
      A. "The strangers"
      B. Means "Sojourners"—"Pilgrims"
      C. Members of churches in several provinces
  III. What's in a Circumstance?
      A. "Scattered throughout"
      B. Literally aliens, refugees, exiles of the Dispersion
      C. Scattered to serve (to become witnesses)

Our Glorious Salvation *(1 Pet. 1:3-12)*
   I. Consider the Hope It Produces (vv. 3-4).
  II. Consider the Assurance It Promises (vv. 4-5).
 III. Consider the Comfort It Provides (vv. 6-7).
 IV. Consider the Completeness It Proclaims (vv. 8-12).

How Sinners Become Saints *(1 Pet. 1:18-19)*
   I. The Power of the Bleeding Savior (v. 19)
  II. The Predicament of Banished Sinners (v. 18*b*)
 III. The Pardoned, Begotten Saints (v. 18*a*)

The Divine Message *(1 Pet. 1:25)*
I. The Author—"The Lord"
II. The Theme—"The Word" that "Endureth"
III. The Method—"Which by the gospel is preached"
IV. The Subjects—"Unto you"
V. The Results—Salvation (implied)

Christ, Our All in All *(1 Pet. 2:24)*
I. Christ, Our Sin Offering
II. Christ, Our Life
III. Christ, Our Righteousness
IV. Christ, Our Healer

Our Great Substitute *(1 Pet. 3:18)*
I. His Sacrifice for Our Sins
   ("Suffered")
II. His Justification for Our Unjustness
   ("Just for the unjust")
III. His Quickening for Our Resurrection
   ("Quickened by the Spirit")

Proper Attitude in Suffering with Christ *(1 Pet. 4:13)*
I. Accept It with Rejoicing.
   A. Trials, though unpleasant, can be helpful.
   B. Trials may bring suffering, but not defeat.
II. Be Glad in It. (Attitude makes the difference.)
   A. We shall be partners in Christ's glory—why not in his suffering?
   B. Considering the future outcome gives comprehension for the present.

The Right and Wrong of Suffering *(1 Pet. 4:14-16)*

I. The Right of It (vv. 14,16)
 A. When it is for Christ, we are following his example.
 B. When it is for Christ, it brings God's approval.
 C. When it is for Christ, he is glorified.

II. The Wrong of It (vv. 14-15)
 A. When it is due to our own evil conduct, it is a bad reflection upon Christ.
 B. When it is due to our own evil conduct, it is dishonoring to God and cannot have his approval.
 C. When it is due to our own evil conduct, the glory due Christ is obscured (v. 14).
 ("On their part he is evil spoken of")

Salvation, Security, Service *(1 Pet. 4:19)*

I. "Let Them" Salvation
 (It is the redeemed that are obedient in suffering.)

II. "Commit the Keeping of Their Souls"—Security
 (It is this blessed assurance by which we trust God in all things.)

III. "As Unto a Faithful Creator"—Service
 (It is in recognition of God's faithfulness that we are moved to faithful service.)

Rewards for Humility *(1 Pet. 5:6)*

I. Humility affords an opportunity for the demonstration of God's power.
 ("The mighty hand of God")

II. Humility affords an opportunity for God to bestow true honor.
("That he may exalt you")
III. Humility affords an opportunity for becoming recipients of God's faithfulness.
("In due time")

The Grace That Perfects *(I Pet. 5:10)*
I. The Action—"Grace"
II. The Availability—"By Christ Jesus"
III. The Accomplishment—"Make you perfect, stablish, strengthen, settle you"

2 PETER

Transformation *Versus* **Reformation** *(2 Pet. 2:20-22)*
I. Reformation is not transformation.
   A. The passage speaks of "knowledge," not cleansing.
   B. This chapter clearly is not referring to saved people (see vv. 1-3).
II. Knowledge without transformation can be deadly.
   A. Dogs and lost souls always return to their old ways.
   B. The latter end is worse with the enlightened sinner than the beginning (see Luke 12:47-48).
III. Believing is experiencing.
   A. Knowledge of the Lord Jesus Christ is not sufficient; it is only a beginning to the way of salvation.
   B. Faith in the Lord Jesus Christ is the only door to salvation (see John 10:9).

Scoffers *(2 Pet. 3:3-7)*
I. Scoffers are basically evil (v. 3).
II. Scoffers deny the doctrine of Christ's literal return (v. 4).
III. Scoffers are ignorant of the ways of God as revealed by the Scriptures (vv. 5-7).
IV. Scoffers are to be judged in "the day of judgment and perdition of ungodly men" (v. 7).

God's Superior Nature *(2 Pet. 3:9)*
  I. "Slackness" is not in God's nature.
  II. "Slackness" is the product of man's sinful nature.
  III. "Longsuffering" is a revelation of God's divine nature.

The Effects of Grace upon the Child of God *(2 Pet. 3:18)*
  I. Position Is Effected.
    (We are growing in the grace in which we stand.)
  II. Learning Is Effected.
    (We are growing in knowledge which we have received.)
  III. Identity Is Effected.
    (We are growing in servitude to our Lord with whom we now have an intimate, spiritual relationship.)
  IV. Outlook Is Effected.
    (We are growing in self-denial as we exalt our Savior.)
    ("To him be glory")

1 JOHN

Your Invitation to Life *(1 John 1:3)*
- I. The Source (authority) for the Invitation
  ("That which we have seen and heard")
- II. The Subject of the Invitation
  ("Fellowship with us")
- III. The Scope of the Invitation
  ("Fellowship is with the Father, and with his Son Jesus Christ")

An Evident Declaration *(1 John 1:3-4)*
- I. The Message Which Was Presented (v. 3a)
  ("That which we have seen and heard")
- II. The Fellowship Which Is Made Possible (v. 3b)
  ("With the Father, and with his Son")
- III. The Joy That Has Been Provided (v. 4)
  ("That your joy may be full")

A Rewarding Declaration *(1 John 1:5-6)*
- I. A Message Received Through Divine Revelation
- II. A Message Retold Through Dedicated Response
- III. A Message to Be Received Through Decisive Reasoning

Victory Over Sin *(1 John 2:1)*
- I. What We Should Do (Abstain)
  ("That ye sin not")
- II. What We Could Do (Possibility)
  ("And if any man sin")

III. What We Must Do (Repent and Confess)
   ("We have an advocate with the Father")

Our Grounds of Security *(1 John 2:1-3)*
   I. The witness of Christ's intercessory presence within us (v. 1)
   II. The witness of Christ's atoning death for us (v. 2)
   III. The witness of Christ's commandments through us (v. 3)

Direction: Bad and Good *(1 John 2:15-17)*
   I. Distorted Devotion (v. 15)
   II. Damaging Deception (vv. 16-17*a*)
   III. Divine Direction (v. 17*b*)

What Manner of Love? *(1 John 3:1)*
   I. An Adopting Love
      ("That we should be called the sons of God")
   II. A Separating Love
      ("Therefore the world knoweth us not")
   III. A Rejected Love
      ("Because it [the world] knew him not")

These Things We Hold *(1 John 3:2-3)*
   I. The Greatest Acclamation Possible (v. 2*a*)
   II. The Greatest Expectation Possible (v. 2*b*)
   III. The Greatest Sanctification Possible (v. 3)

Perceiving God's Love *(1 John 3:16-19)*
  I. God's love provides for us (v. 16a).
  II. God's love through us provides for our brethren (vv. 16b-17).
  III. True charity growing out of God's love assures our hearts before him.

The Spirit of Antichrist *(1 John 4:1-3)*
  I. A Sure Warning to Be Heeded (v. 1)
  II. A Sound Test to Be Administered (vv. 2-3a)
  III. A Satanic Presence to Be Avoided (v. 3b)

Our Security in the Godhead *(1 John 4:13-15)*
  I. The Security of the Spirit's Presence (v. 13)
  II. The Security of the Son's Presence (v. 14)
  III. The Security of the Father's Presence (v. 15)

A Great Affirmation *(1 John 4:14-15)*
  I. The Greatest Testimony Ever Given (v. 14a)
  II. The Greatest Need Ever Revealed (v. 14b)
  III. The Greatest Relationship Ever Made Possible (v. 15)

The Evidence of Salvation *(1 John 5:1-2)*
  I. The Evidence of Faith (v. 1a)
  II. The Evidence of Birth (v. 1b)
  III. The Evidence of Charity (v. 2)

Victory Over the World *(1 John 5:4-5)*
　I. Victory Because of Birth (v. 4*a*)
　II. Victory Because of Faith (v. 4*b*)
　III. Victory Because of Association (v. 5)
　　"Jesus is the Son of God."

The Threefold Witness *(1 John 5:10)*
　I. The Credible Witness
　　("The witness in himself")
　II. The Condemning Witness
　　("He that believeth not God")
　III. The Crowning Witness
　　("The record that God gave of his Son")

A Great Revelation *(1 John 5:11-12)*
　I. The Authority for the Revelation
　　(The Word)
　II. The Subject of the Revelation
　　(Eternal life)
　III. The Means of Appropriating the Revelation
　　(Faith in Jesus Christ)
　IV. The Assurance Given by the Revelation
　　("He that hath the Son hath life")
　V. The Tragedy Revealed by the Revelation
　　("He that hath not the Son of God hath not life")

Separation from the World *(1 John 5:19)*
　I. God is our salvation from the curse upon the world.
　II. God is our sanctuary from the cares of the world.
　III. God is our separation from the call of the world.

Rewards of Christ's Presence *(1 John 5:20)*
   I. Godward Knowledge
  II. God-Given Understanding
 III. God-Centered Preparation
 IV. God-Granted Salvation

2 JOHN

A Call to Unity *(2 John 4-11)*
    I. Unity in Truth (v. 4)
    II. Unity in Love (v. 5)
    III. Unity in Sound Doctrine (vv. 7-9)
    IV. Unity in Denouncing False Teachers (vv. 11-12)

Faithfulness to the Word *(2 John 6-9)*
    I. Love of scriptural truth will annul false doctrine.
    II. Love of scriptural truth will bring a full reward.
    III. Love of scriptural truth will purge the heart of all
        doubt.

The Doctrine of Christ *(2 John 9)*
    I. It is the measuring rod of salvation.
    II. It is a curse to skeptics.
    III. It is a blessing to multitudes.
    IV. It is an unchangeable rule.

A Divine Caution *(2 John 11)*
    I. To *commend* evil is to *condone* evil.
    II. To *praise* evil is to *promote* evil.
    III. To *bless* evil is to *become* evil.
    IV. To *reject* evil is to *reduce* evil.

3 JOHN

Marks of a Good Man *(3 John 1-6)*
   I. Full of Truth (vv. 1-4)
  II. Genuine Faithfulness (v. 5)
 III. A Good Testimony (v. 6)

Godless Pride *(3 John 9-10)*
    I. Godless pride can hinder God's will.
   II. Godless pride can hinder God's servants.
  III. Godless pride can hinder the work of the church.
  IV. Godless pride hinders the sinner from finding God
       (v. 11).
    ("He that doeth evil hath not seen God.")

The Value of a Good Report *(3 John 11-12)*
   I. It brings the respect of men (v. 12).
    ("Good report of all men")
  II. It establishes a reputation of integrity (v. 12).
   ("Of truth itself")
 III. It gives evidence of true godliness (v. 11).
   ("He that doeth good is of God")

JUDE

Jude's Description of Perfect Christianity *(Jude 20-23)*
  I. Constant Growth in Faith (v. 20)
  II. Constant Spiritual Praying (v. 20)
  III. Constant Walking in the Love of God (v. 21)
  IV. Constant Patience in the Hope of Glory (v. 21)
  V. Constant Compassion Toward the Unsaved (v. 22)
  VI. Constant Hatred for the Sins of the Flesh (v. 23)

The Upward Way *(Jude 20-23)*
  I. Building Up (v. 20)
  II. Keeping Up (v. 21*a*)
  III. Looking Up (v. 21*b*)
  IV. Lifting Up (v. 22)
  V. Pulling Up (v. 23)

Our Stand in Christ *(Jude 24)*
  I. In Christ We Are FAIL-SAFE.
  II. In Christ We Are FAULTLESS.
  III. In Christ We Are FAVORED.

REVELATION

The Great Appearance *(Rev. 1:7)*
   I. The Great Foretelling
      ("Behold, he cometh with clouds.")
  II. The Great Unveiling
      ("Every eye shall see him.")
 III. The Great Wailing
      ("All kindreds of the earth shall wail because of
        him.")

Revelation: The Unveiled Christ
    I. The Eternal One (1:17-18)
   II. The Lion of the Tribe of Judah (5:5)
  III. The Lamb Endowed with Honor, Glory, and Power
      (5:12-13)
  IV. The King of This World (11:15)
   V. The Judge and the Commander of Heaven's Army
      (19:11)
  VI. The Gracious Lord of the New Creation (21:5-7)
 VII. The Supreme Character of the Drama of All Divine
      Revelation (22:16)

Christ at the Door *(Rev. 3:20)*
  I. Every Heart Has a Door.
    A. It is a door that blocks the entrance of Christ
      (old nature).
    B. It is a door that offers great possibilities (new
      nature).
 II. Every Person Is the Keeper of His Heart's Door.
    A. Will keeps the door closed to Christ.

B. Will alone can open the door to Christ.
III. Every Invitation Has a Condition ("If").
    A. "If" one wants the salvation Christ offers
    B. "If" one wants the blessings which Christ's presence will bring

The Persistence of Christ *(Rev. 3:20)*

  I. Christ Signals.
    (He knocks—lets his presence be known)
  II. Christ Speaks.
    ("Hear my voice")
  III. Christ Seeks.
    (To "come in")
  IV. Christ Sups.
    (With those who open the door to him)

The Conquering Beast *(Rev. 13:4-7)*

  I. The Antichristian Beast (v. 4)
  II. The Arrogant Beast (vv. 5-6)
  III. The Angry Beast (v. 7)
  IV. The Avenging Beast (v. 7)

The Bride of Christ *(Rev. 19:7-9)*

  I. Her Gladness (v. 7*a*)
  II. Her Grooming (v. 7*b*)
  III. Her Grant (v. 8*a*)
  IV. Her Glory (v. 8*b*)
  V. Her Guarantee (v. 9)

Armageddon's Bloody Victory *(Rev. 19:11-21)*
  I. Behold the Blood-Robed King (v. 13)
  II. Behold the Blood-Washed Saints (v. 14)
  III. Behold the Blood-Drenched Enemy (v. 21*a*)
  IV. Behold the Blood-Fetid Banquet (v. 21*b*)

Some Crowns of Christ *(Rev. 19:12)*
"And on his head were many crowns."
  I. The Crown He Sacrificed
     (heavenly crown) (Gal. 4:4)
  II. The Crown He Chose
      (crown of thorns) (Matt. 27:29)
  III. The Crown He Gained
       (crown of glory) (Heb. 2:9)

The End of All Evil *(Rev. 20:10)*
  I. This Will Be the End of Deception.
  II. This Will Be the End of the Deceiver.
  III. This Will Be the End of All Deceptive Devices.

The Great Judgment Throne *(Rev. 20:11-15)*
  I. Consider the Place of the Throne.
  II. Consider the Parity of the Throne.
  III. Consider the Person on the Throne.
  IV. Consider the People Before the Throne.
  V. Consider the Purpose of the Throne.
  VI. Consider the Pronouncement from the Throne.

The Great Judgment *(Rev. 20:11-15)*
    I. The Great Throne (v. 11)
    II. The Great Throng (vv. 12-13)
    III. The Great Tragedy (v. 14)
    IV. The Great Torment (v. 15)
        (Compare v. 10)

Eternity's New Things *(Rev. 21:1-4)*
    I. A New Heaven (v. 1)
    II. A New Earth (v. 1)
    III. A New City (v. 2)
    IV. A New Tabernacle (v. 3)
    V. A New Dimension (v. 4)

Seven Heavenly Wonders *(Rev. 21:1-5,22-27; 22:1-5)*
    I. Its Renowned Company
    II. Its Remarkable Immunity
    III. Its Resplendent Purity
    IV. Its Revealing Identity
    V. Its Refreshing Activity
    VI. Its Rewarding Eternity
    VII. Its Radiant Glory

A Great Glimpse of the Future *(Rev. 21:3)*
    I. The Great Heavenly Proclamation
    II. The Great Involvement of God with His People
    III. The Great Time of Worship in Which We Shall Participate

A Promise and a Prediction *(Rev. 21:7-8)*
    I. This speaks to all people of the importance of preparedness.
    II. This promises provision for the prepared.
    III. This predicts perdition for the unprepared.

The City of God *(Rev. 21:27)*
    I. The Sanctions Imposed
    II. The Sacredness Disclosed
    III. The Separated Exposed

Heaven *(Rev. 22:3)*
    I. Heaven, Place of Delivered Souls
    II. Heaven, Place of Divine Presence
    III. Heaven, Place of Delightful Service

The Day of the Lord *(Rev. 22:10-12)*
    I. The final warning issued regarding the impending day of the Lord (v. 10)
    ("For the time is at hand")
    II. The finality of the ungodliness of the godless in the day of the Lord (v. 11*a*)
    ("He that is unjust, let him be unjust still")
    III. The finality of the righteousness of the righteous in the day of the Lord (v. 11*b*)
    ("He that is righteous, let him be righteous still")

The Three Great and Final Warnings of the Bible *(Rev. 22:17-20)*

   I. The warning of the approaching last invitation (v. 17)

  II. The warning against tampering with divine prophecy (vv. 18-19)

 III. The warning of Christ's unannounced and sudden return (v. 20)

Revelation's Prophetic Warning *(Rev. 22:18-19)*

   I. We Must Respect the Sanctity of "This Prophecy."

  II. We Must Realize the Seriousness of "This Prophecy."

 III. We Must Relish the Sealing of "This Prophecy."